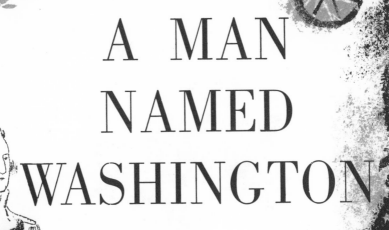

A MAN
NAMED
WASHINGTON

By Gertrude Norman

Illustrated by James Caraway

G. P. Putnam's Sons   New York

© 1960 by Gertrude Norman
Illustrations © 1960 by James Caraway

Library of Congress Catalog Card Number: 60-5640
Manufactured in the United States of America
Published simultaneously in the Dominion of Canada by
Longmans, Green and Company, Toronto.

A long time ago—
There was a boy named
    George Washington.
He lived on a big farm, with a lot
    of land,
And fields, and tall trees near the house.

George liked to ride his pony
    around the farm,
And talk to the men who worked
    for his father.
They took care of the land
    and grew food,
And looked after the animals—the
    cows, pigs, and chickens.

George had a big brother.
His name was Larry.
But George did not know Larry,
Because he was far away, across the sea,
    in England.

Every night George's mother told him
 a story.
"England is far away," said his mother.
"Long ago men came here
 from England.
They came across the sea to America,
 to stay.
Then more men and women came.
Their children grew up and
 had children here.
So you see—now we live in America."

"Tell me about England," said George.

"There is a king in England,"
    said his mother.
"He is our king, too.
He makes the laws for us.
We must do as he says."

"I want to see Larry," said George.
"Oh, you will," said his mother.
"He will come home one day,
    to America."

George went to school. He learned
    to read,

And write his name—
    GEORGE WASHINGTON,
And add—3 + 3 = 6.
He played with the other boys at school,
And grew tall and strong.

When his father gave him a horse
    for his birthday,
He was very happy.
"I'll gallop all over the farm," he said.

One day a big, grown-up man came
        to the door.
It was Larry!
"I am a soldier," said Larry.

"In England a soldier wears a red coat."
He showed George his gun and his coat.
"Some day you may be a soldier, too,"
        he said.

George was still a boy when his
        father died.
Then he went to live on Larry's farm,
He learned to ride in the woods,
He learned about land,
How to measure it and make a map of it.

One day a rich man came to see Larry.
"I have a lot of land," he said.
"It is far away, in the deep woods.
I must send some men to measure
    this land
Because I want to sell it.
Do you know any men who would
    like to go?"

"I want to go," said George.
I am sixteen now. I am grown-up."

George rode away with the men,
Far away into the deep woods.
They cooked their food over a fire,
And slept in a tent at night.

George liked to see the sun on the trees,
And hear the birds sing,
As he helped the men measure the land.

One dark, cold night, it rained hard.
Some Indians came running to the fire.
They danced around the fire to
      get warm.
"I never saw Indians before,"
      said George.

When George came home, the
    rich man said,
"You did good work. I will pay
    you well
And give you some land to keep."

George went back to the woods
    many times,
And made friends with the Indians.
"Oh White Man," they said,
"You are brave and strong like us,
You know the woods like an Indian."

At home George learned to be a soldier,
Larry showed him and his friends –
                    how to march,
                    to fall in line,
                    to hold a gun,
                    and shoot on
                          horseback.

George worked hard.
He measured a lot of land.
Soon he had the money
To buy more land of his own.

One day Larry galloped up—
"Some Indians are fighting the
    White Men," he said,
"And the King has sent soldiers
    from England.
We must go far away and help them
    fight the Indians.
Tell your friends—Hurry! Get ready!"

The Indians knew how to fight
    in the woods,
They would climb the tall trees
And shoot down on the Redcoats
    from England.

George knew how to fight like
   an Indian.
He was very brave.
When his horse was killed,
He found another horse and
   went on fighting.

Everyone looked up to him,
Because he was such a fine soldier,
And when the head of the Army died,
George became the head.

The Indians lost the war
And George went home.
Then Larry died and left
George his farm,
Named Mount Vernon,
A fine, big farm on a hill.

One night George went to a party
And danced with a young woman.
Her name was Martha.
"How pretty you are!" said George.

He went to see her many times.
"Will you marry me?" he said.
        "Will you be my wife?"
"Yes," said Martha, "I will be your wife."

So Martha came to live at
        Mount Vernon.
They had a fine house and a
        lot of land.
It was such a happy time for
        George and Martha.

But then a bad time came for America.

There was a new king in England
And he made new laws for America.
He wanted the Americans to pay him
    more money.
The Americans did not like these laws.
They would not do what the King said.

"I will send my soldiers," the
    King shouted.
"The Americans must do as I say."

Then a lot of men met in America,
In city, town, and farm,
And talked about what to do.
"The King is not fair to us," they said,
"And we may have to fight England."

Then George said,
"Peace is better than war,
But we will fight, if we have to,
And show the King we are brave."

Everyone loved George,
They heard great things about him.

"We must go to war," said the men,
"For there is no other way.
We will show the King
That we can make our own laws.
And George will lead us in this war,
For he is our best soldier.
He will be the head of our Army."

Soon George said good-by to Martha
And rode away to lead the Army.

Now big boats came from England—
The Redcoats had a lot of guns,
And food, and warm clothes,
And everything they needed.

But the Americans were not ready.
Some soldiers had no guns.
Some had no warm clothes, or shoes.
They had to fight in the snow
        without shoes.
Many of them were hungry.

George stayed next to his soldiers
And tried to help them.
He wanted more guns for his men,
And warm clothes, and better food.
He was kind to his soldiers,
And so brave that they were brave, too.

The war went on and on.
George said, "We will not give up,
We will find a way to win."

One Christmas,
      the Redcoats camped on one side
         of a river,
      and George's Army camped on
         the other side.
      It was very very cold.
      But the Redcoats had a party.
      They were happy,
      Because it was Christmas.

George's soldiers were cold and hungry,
As they waited in the ice and snow
Till the Redcoats went to sleep.
Then George led his men across
        the river,
Across the deep ice and snow.
What a surprise for the Redcoats,
When they woke up and were captured.
What a fine day for George!

The war went on,
Till at last the Red coats said,
"We cannot win. We give up."

So the war was over,
And everyone was happy.
Boys and girls danced in the street,
Old men and women, too.
America was free, now,
Free to make its own laws.

George went back to Mount Vernon
And gave Martha a hug.
"Now I will stay here with you,"
    he said.

But everyone said, "No.
There is much to do in America.
We do not want a king,
But we must have a leader,
And good men to make our laws.
The best man is George Washington.
He was great in time of war.
He will be great in time of peace."

Then George became President
And worked with other men,
To rule America without a king,
And make laws that were fair to all.

Everyone said, "Our President is great."

Near Mount Vernon, a new city
        was built.
And it was named Washington.

On his birthday—February 22nd—
We think of George Washington,
Who became our first President.

New Words in This Book

against	march
army	marry
became	measure
born	need
brave	paper
camp	peace
capture	president
died	rich
fight	rule
free	shoot
law	soldiers
leader	strong
map	war

young